CARNIVORES

Heather C. Hudak

MEDIA ENHANCED BOOKS
AV2 BY WEIGL™
ADDED VALUE • AUDIO VISUAL

www.av2books.com

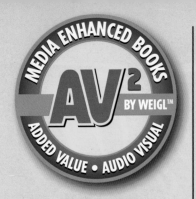

AV² provides enriched content that supplements and complements this book. Weigl's AV² books strive to create inspired learning and engage young minds in a total learning experience.

Your AV² Media Enhanced books come alive with...

Audio
Listen to sections of the book read aloud.

Key Words
Study vocabulary, and complete a matching word activity.

Video
Watch informative video clips.

Quizzes
Test your knowledge.

Embedded Weblinks
Gain additional information for research.

Slide Show
View images and captions, and prepare a presentation.

Try This!
Complete activities and hands-on experiments.

Go to **www.av2books.com**, and enter this book's unique code.

BOOK CODE

L 5 0 1 3 7 6

AV² **by Weigl** brings you media enhanced books that support active learning.

... and much, much more!

Published by AV² by Weigl
350 5th Avenue, 59th Floor
New York, NY 10118
Website: www.av2books.com   www.weigl.com

Library of Congress Cataloging-in-Publication Data

Hudak, Heather C., 1975-
 Carnivores / Heather C. Hudak.
   p. cm. — (Food chains)
 Includes index.
 ISBN 978-1-61690-707-5 (hardcover: alk. paper) — ISBN 978-1-61690-713-6 (softcover: alk. paper)
1. Carnivora—Juvenile literature. I. Title.
 QL737.C2H83 2011
 591.5'3—dc22   2010050994

Printed in the United States of America in North Mankato, Minnesota
1 2 3 4 5 6 7 8 9 0 15 14 13 12 11

062011
WEP290411

Project Coordinator Aaron Carr
Art Director Terry Paulhus

Photo Credits
Every reasonable effort has been made to trace ownership and to obtain permission to reprint copyright material. The publishers would be pleased to have any errors or omissions brought to their attention so that they may be corrected in subsequent printings.

Weigl acknowledges Getty Images as its primary image supplier for this title.

Contents

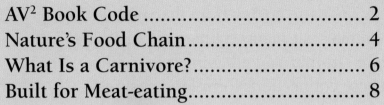

Nature's Food Chain

All living things need food to survive. Food provides the **energy** that plants and animals need to grow and thrive.

Plants and animals do not rely on the same types of food to live. Plants make their own food. They use energy from the Sun and water from the soil. Some animals eat plants. Others eat animals that have already eaten plants. In this way, all living things are connected to each other. These connections form food chains.

A food chain is made up of **producers** and **consumers**. Plants are the main producers in a food chain. This is because they make energy. This energy can be used by the rest of the living things on Earth. The other living things are called consumers.

There are five types of consumers in a food chain. They are carnivores, decomposers, herbivores, omnivores, and parasites. All of the world's organisms belong to one of these groups in the food chain.

Hawks use their razor-sharp claws to kill animals such as mice, snakes, and other birds.

Chain Reactions

If an animal's food source disappears, other animals will suffer and possibly die.

FOOD CHAIN

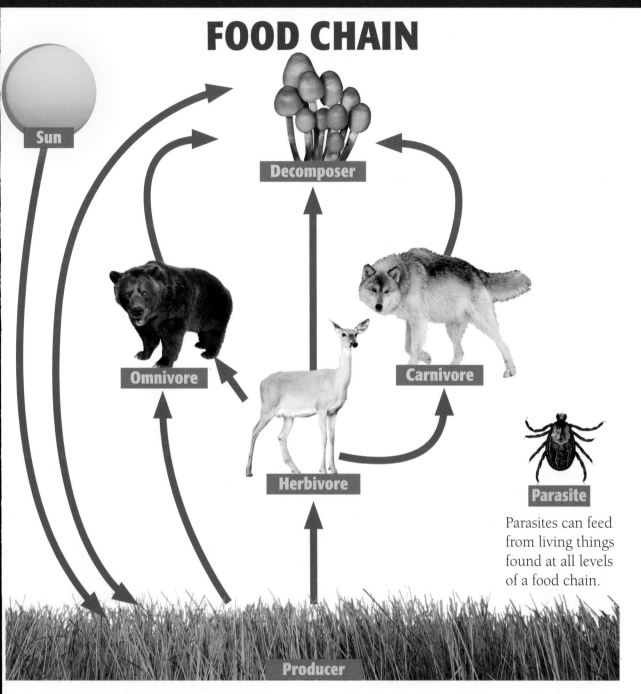

Parasites can feed from living things found at all levels of a food chain.

In this example, the Sun starts the food chain by providing energy for grass to grow. The deer eats grass as its food, and the wolf eats the deer. Bears may also eat grass or deer. Mushrooms receive energy from grass and the waste left behind by wolves, deer, and bears. Parasites can be found at any point along the food chain. They can live inside or on producers and consumers. A tick can get the food it needs to survive from a deer, a bear, or a wolf.

What Is a Carnivore?

Carnivore means "meat-eater." It is a Latin word. The term carnivore describes animals in the food chain that eat the flesh of other animals. Carnivores get their energy from eating the meat of other living things. Most carnivores eat herbivores.

Herbivores are plant-eating animals. Some carnivores eat omnivores. Omnivores are animals that eat both plants and meat. Many carnivores hunt and kill their own **prey**. Some carnivores eat dead animals. Cheetahs, crocodiles, great white sharks, weasels, and wolves are all examples of carnivores. Some insects and birds are also carnivores.

Crocodiles live in rivers, lakes, and wetlands. They eat many kinds of fish.

Carnivores hunt their food. They must eat a large number of **calories** so they have enough energy to hunt. Some carnivores, such as wolves and some dolphins, hunt as a group. It is easier for a group to catch large prey. The animals in the group share the catch.

Other carnivores, such as lynx, wait for prey to come near. Then they pounce on the prey. This is called lie-and-wait hunting. Some carnivores that lie and wait for prey are camouflaged. This means they blend into their environment. Some carnivores attract prey to them. For example, the viperfish has 350 tiny lights inside its mouth. These lights act as a lure, or bait. Once prey are near, the viperfish uses its long sharp teeth to grab its food.

Occasionally, a wolf will hunt on its own. A wolf can catch smaller animals, such as beavers, birds, rabbits, and raccoons.

Largest Carnivore

The polar bear is the largest land carnivore. Most polar bears weigh more than 700 pounds (320 kilograms).

Built for Meat-eating

All carnivores have features that are **adapted** to their diets. Many carnivores have special body parts that help them chew meat and obtain the energy they need from it.

Among the most important body features for all carnivores are the teeth. Carnivore teeth are designed for eating meat. Carnivores have short, pointed **incisors** for nipping and biting. They have sharp **canines** for stabbing and holding prey. Carnivores have **premolars**. These teeth are used for cutting and slicing flesh. Carnivores have **molars** for grinding and crushing bones.

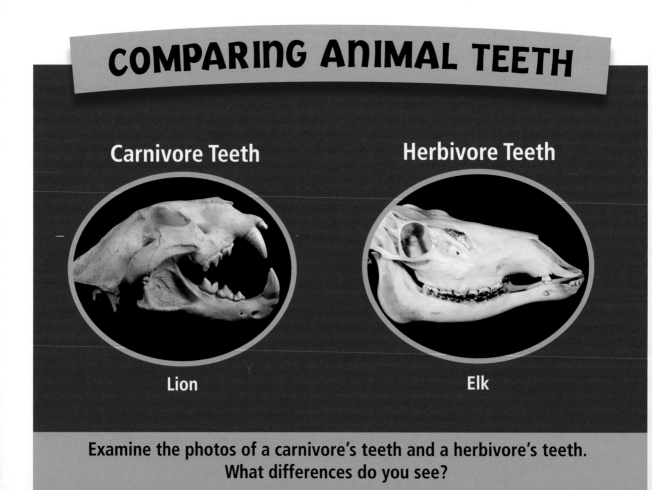

COMPARING ANIMAL TEETH

Carnivore Teeth

Lion

Herbivore Teeth

Elk

Examine the photos of a carnivore's teeth and a herbivore's teeth. What differences do you see?

Most carnivores have very keen senses. Senses help them locate their prey. Felines, or cats, can see very well. During the day, they see about the same quality as humans. At night, a part of a cat's eye opens wide to let more light shine through. This allows cats to see well in the dark.

Felines can hear well, too. They can turn their ears to hear even the quietest sounds. This feature helps them know the type and size of prey in their environment. Some carnivores have a very keen sense of smell. Hyenas and dingoes use their sense of smell to track prey.

Most cats are active at night. They use their excellent night vision to hunt and capture their prey in the dark.

JAWS

The jaws of many carnivores move up and down. This helps them tear and bite meat.

Ravenous Reptiles

Many different kinds of reptiles are carnivores. Reptiles eat eggs, insects, and small **vertebrates**, such as **amphibians**, birds, fish, **rodents**, and other reptiles. Carnivorous reptiles catch prey in many ways. Most reptiles, such as alligators and snakes, have sharp teeth. Some reptiles have long claws. Komodo dragons use their claws to grab and rip their prey. This allows them to eat large animals such as goats, monkeys, and wild pigs.

The komodo dragon has deadly substances in its saliva. When a komodo dragon bites its prey, these substances can kill the victim within a week.

Boa constrictors do not have claws. Instead, a boa wraps its body tightly around the prey. After some time, the prey can no longer breathe. When the prey dies, the boa swallows the entire animal, head first. Boas can stretch their jaws wide open to swallow animals much larger than their heads.

Another type of carnivorous reptile is the crocodile. This large animal has thirty to forty teeth on each jaw. These teeth fit together when the crocodile closes its mouth. Crocodiles swim underwater with just their nostrils and eyes above the surface. They sneak up on their prey. Then they drag the animal underwater and hold it until it drowns. Crocodiles can crush small animals by snapping their mouths closed on the animal.

Jacobson's Organ

Most reptiles have a Jacobson's organ in their mouth. This organ helps reptiles taste and smell. They use the Jacobson's organ to hunt prey, find mates, and know what is in their surroundings.

Creepy Crawlies

There are more than 40,000 **species** of spiders. All spiders are carnivorous. They eat insects, other spiders, and small vertebrates, such as birds and frogs. There are two types of spiders. Ground spiders hunt their prey. Web spiders spin webs to catch prey. Most spiders use venom, or poison, to kill or **paralyze** their prey before eating it.

A web spider's body produces an oil that prevents it from getting stuck to its own web.

Tarantulas are large, hairy spiders. Most tarantulas live in **tropical** regions. They eat insects and other small animals. Tarantulas do not spin webs. They use speed and strength to sneak up on their prey. Then, they pounce on the prey and bite it with their fangs. Unlike other carnivores, tarantulas do not have teeth for chewing. They can only drink their food. Tarantulas inject their prey with substances that turn the prey's insides into liquid. The tarantula sucks this liquid and leaves the prey's body behind.

Tarantulas have small hairs on their belly that they rub on their predators. This distracts the predators so the tarantula can escape.

Ouch!

Spiders stab their prey with long, pointed teeth called fangs. The fangs are located on the front of a spider's mouth. Poison is released from the tip of the fang into the prey.

Carnivore Close-ups

There are many kinds of carnivores. They come in all shapes and sizes. Some of the world's largest and smallest animals are carnivores. Carnivores can be found throughout the world. Some carnivores live in water. Many live on land.

Cheetah

+ fastest land animal
+ lives in Africa
+ reaches speeds of 70 miles per hour (113 kilometers per hour)
+ hunts during the day
+ can live without water for long periods of time, because it gathers much of the water it needs from the body fluids of its prey
+ eats gazelles, hares, and impala

Swift Fox

+ smallest canine, or dog, in North America
+ grows to be about 12 inches (30 centimeters) high
+ lives in open spaces in North America
+ reaches speeds of 25 miles per hour (40 kilometers per hour)
+ eats amphibians, birds, small mammals, and reptiles

Blue Whale

- largest animal on Earth; grows to more than 80 feet (24 meters) long
- travels from tropical oceans in winter to **pack ice** in summer
- uses baleens, or horn-like material in the mouth, to filter prey from water
- lunges open-mouthed into schools of fish, krill, or plankton

Peregrine Falcon

- fastest bird
- reaches speeds between 180 and 200 miles per hour (290 and 320 kilometers per hour)
- hunts by snatching prey in flight using its sharp talons, or claws
- uses a sharp, tooth-like point on its beak to tear apart prey
- eats frogs, insects, rodents, and small birds, such as ducks, pigeons, and seabirds

Least Weasel

- smallest mammal carnivore
- grows to be about 4 to 10 inches (10 to 25 centimeters) long
- lives on farmland and in wooded areas
- can kill animals up to five times its size
- uses its claws and sharp teeth to catch prey
- eats small birds, mice, moles, rabbits, and rats

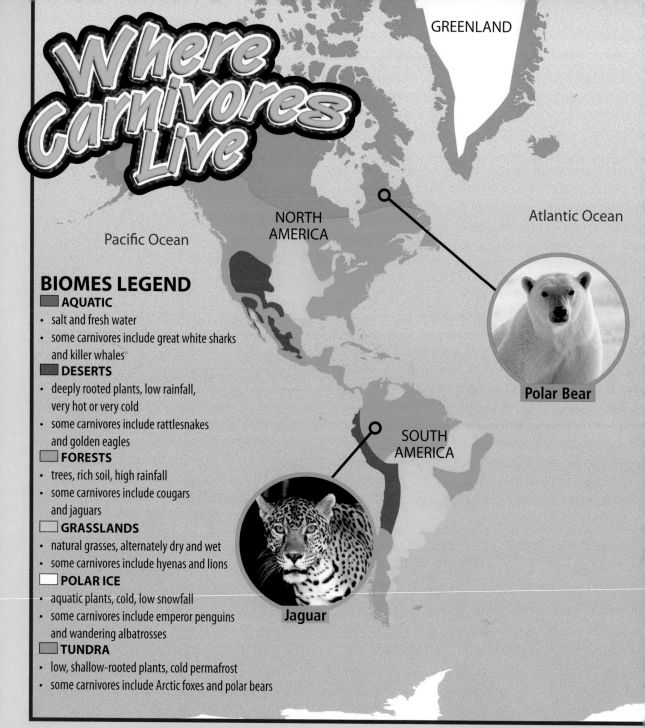

Where Carnivores Live

GREENLAND

NORTH AMERICA

Atlantic Ocean

Pacific Ocean

Polar Bear

SOUTH AMERICA

Jaguar

BIOMES LEGEND

AQUATIC
- salt and fresh water
- some carnivores include great white sharks and killer whales

DESERTS
- deeply rooted plants, low rainfall, very hot or very cold
- some carnivores include rattlesnakes and golden eagles

FORESTS
- trees, rich soil, high rainfall
- some carnivores include cougars and jaguars

GRASSLANDS
- natural grasses, alternately dry and wet
- some carnivores include hyenas and lions

POLAR ICE
- aquatic plants, cold, low snowfall
- some carnivores include emperor penguins and wandering albatrosses

TUNDRA
- low, shallow-rooted plants, cold permafrost
- some carnivores include Arctic foxes and polar bears

All carnivores require special living conditions in order to thrive. The place where an animal lives is called its habitat. Earth has many different **biomes** that serve as habitats. Biomes are defined by their climates and by the plants and animals that live there. The world's largest biomes are aquatic, deserts, forests, grasslands, polar ice, and tundra.

A carnivore's habitat can be as big as a desert or a forest. It can also be as small as a tree branch or a pond. Each carnivore must live where it can get the food it needs to survive. Killer whales live in the aquatic biome. They eat a

Arctic Ocean

Golden Eagle

ASIA

EUROPE

Pacific Ocean

AFRICA

Indian Ocean

Killer Whale

AUSTRALIA

Southern Ocean

Lion

SCALE

1,250 Miles

0   2,000 Kilometers

N
W — E
S

ANTARCTICA

variety of marine mammals, seabirds, squid, and fish. They would not live long on grasslands.

A carnivore that lives in a biome in one part of the world might not live in the same biome in a different part of the world. For example, jaguars live in the forests of South America but not in the forests of Europe.

Look at the map to see where some types of carnivores may live. Can you think of other carnivores? Where on the map do they live?

Carnivores at Risk

Plants and animals rely on each other in order to survive. For example, carnivores eat herbivores that live in a region. Sometimes the carnivore moves to a new region or becomes **extinct**. If this happens, the herbivore population grows. The herbivores overeat the plants in the region. Over time, there will not be enough plant materials for the herbivores to eat.

Another example is sea otters that eat sea urchins. Without sea otters, sea urchins overeat the kelp or seaweed in the region. This means other plants and animals, such as fish and seabirds, cannot thrive. If there were no sea otters, kelp would die. If there were no kelp, fish and seabirds would die.

Sea otters swim on their backs, using their bellies to balance and carry food.

When a carnivore's habitat is destroyed and food is no longer available, that carnivore becomes **endangered**. Every day, carnivores, from insects to mammals, become endangered or extinct. An endangered carnivore puts herbivores and plants at risk, too.

In most cases, humans cause the world's plants and animals to become endangered. When people clear land to build communities or grow crops, many plants and animals lose their homes and their food supplies. Some environmental groups work to preserve the world's natural habitats.

ZOOLOGIST

Career
A zoologist is a scientist who studies animals. Zoologists study how animals grow and develop, as well as how they behave and interact with other animals.

Education
A minimum of a bachelor's degree is required in biology or another area of science. For many jobs, a master's or doctorate degree is needed. Strong math and computer skills are also important.

Working Conditions
Zoologists work in a range of environments. Much of their research is done in nature, but many zoologists also conduct experiments in laboratories and at zoos.

Tools
Field Equipment: binoculars, camera, video camera, audio recorder, pencil, sketchbook, maps, global positioning system (GPS) device
Lab Equipment: computer, scalpels, tweezers, microscope

Endangered Species

The snow leopard is endangered. It lives at altitudes higher than 19,000 feet (6,000 meters). This animal's solitary nature and remote habitat make it difficult for scientists to see and study snow leopards.

Making an Energy Pyramid

A food chain is one way to chart the transfer of energy from one living thing to another. Another way to show how living things are connected is through an energy pyramid. An energy pyramid starts with the Sun. The Sun provides the energy that allows producers to grow. Producers are a source of energy for primary consumers in the next level of the pyramid. Primary consumers transfer energy up the pyramid to tertiary consumers. In this way, all living things depend on one another for survival. In the example below, grass is food for rabbits, and rabbits are food for wolves.

ENERGY PYRAMID

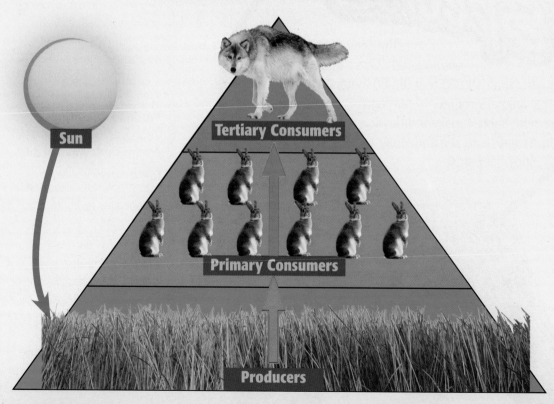

Sun

Tertiary Consumers

Primary Consumers

Producers

Below are some examples of carnivores and the habitat where they live. Choose one of the animals and learn more about it. Using the Internet and your school library, find information about the animal's diet. Determine which animals the carnivore might eat. Using your carnivore as the tertiary consumer, draw an energy pyramid showing the transfer of energy. Which primary consumers are a source of energy for the animal you picked? Which producers are a source of energy for the primary consumers in your energy pyramid?

CARNIVORES

AQUATIC	Jellyfish	Sea Otter	Dolphin
DESERTS	Barn Owl	Gila Monster	Bobcat
FORESTS	Cougar	Spider	Frog
GRASSLANDS	Crocodile	Dragonfly	Marabou Stork
TUNDRA	Peregrine Falcon	Arctic Fox	Penguin

Quick Quiz

Based on what you have just read, try to answer the following questions correctly.

1. What does the word carnivore mean?

2. What is the largest carnivore on Earth?

3. How many teeth do crocodiles have?

4. What is the smallest carnivorous mammal?

5. What is the name of an endangered cat species?

6. How do tarantulas eat their food?

7. What do sea otters eat?

8. How do a carnivore's jaws move to help it tear meat?

Answers: 1. Meat-eater **2.** The blue whale **3.** 30 to 40 in each jaw **4.** The least weasel **5.** The snow leopard **6.** They turn their prey into liquid and suck the liquid through their mouth **7.** Sea urchins **8.** Up and down

Glossary

adapted: changed over time to fit an environment

amphibians: cold-blooded animals with smooth skin that spend part of their life on land and part in water

biomes: large areas with the same climate and other natural conditions in which certain kinds of plants and animals live

calories: units that measure the amount of energy a food produces when taken into the body

canines: pointed teeth located between the front and back teeth

consumers: animals that feed on plants or other animals

endangered: at risk of no longer living any place on Earth

energy: the usable power living things receive from food that they use to grow, move, and stay healthy

extinct: no longer living any place on Earth

incisors: front teeth used for cutting and gnawing

molars: large teeth used for grinding food

pack ice: a solid mass of floating ice covering a wide area, especially in polar regions

paralyze: to take away the ability to move

premolars: teeth located before the molars

prey: animals that are hunted by other animals for food

producers: living things, such as plants, that produce their own food

rodents: animals that have a pair of big front teeth used for gnawing

species: a group of the same kind of living thing; members can breed together

tropical: areas that have a very warm climate year-round

vertebrates: animals that have a backbone

Log on to www.av2books.com

AV² by Weigl brings you media enhanced books that support active learning. Go to www.av2books.com, and enter the special code found on page 2 of this book. You will gain access to enriched and enhanced content that supplements and complements this book. Content includes video, audio, web links, quizzes, a slide show, and activities.

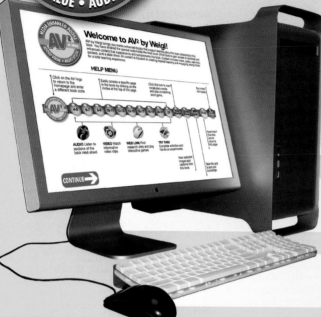

Audio
Listen to sections of the book read aloud.

Video
Watch informative video clips.

Embedded Weblinks
Gain additional information for research.

Try This!
Complete activities and hands-on experiments.

WHAT'S ONLINE?

Try This!	Embedded Weblinks	Video	EXTRA FEATURES
Test your knowledge of food chains.	Discover more carnivores.	Watch a video introduction to carnivores.	**Audio** Listen to sections of the book read aloud.
Outline the features of an carnivore.	Learn more about one of the carnivores in this book.	Watch a video about a carnivore.	**Key Words** Study vocabulary, and complete a matching word activity.
Research a carnivore.	Find out more about carnivore conservation efforts.		
Compare carnivores that live in different areas.	Learn more about carnivores.		**Slide Show** View images and captions, and prepare a presentation
Try an interactive activity.			**Quizzes** Test your knowledge.

AV² was built to bridge the gap between print and digital. We encourage you to tell us what you like and what you want to see in the future.

Sign up to be an AV² Ambassador at www.av2books.com/ambassador.

Glossary

adapted: changed over time to fit an environment

amphibians: cold-blooded animals with smooth skin that spend part of their life on land and part in water

biomes: large areas with the same climate and other natural conditions in which certain kinds of plants and animals live

calories: units that measure the amount of energy a food produces when taken into the body

canines: pointed teeth located between the front and back teeth

consumers: animals that feed on plants or other animals

endangered: at risk of no longer living any place on Earth

energy: the usable power living things receive from food that they use to grow, move, and stay healthy

extinct: no longer living any place on Earth

incisors: front teeth used for cutting and gnawing

molars: large teeth used for grinding food

pack ice: a solid mass of floating ice covering a wide area, especially in polar regions

paralyze: to take away the ability to move

premolars: teeth located before the molars

prey: animals that are hunted by other animals for food

producers: living things, such as plants, that produce their own food

rodents: animals that have a pair of big front teeth used for gnawing

species: a group of the same kind of living thing; members can breed together

tropical: areas that have a very warm climate year-round

vertebrates: animals that have a backbone

Index

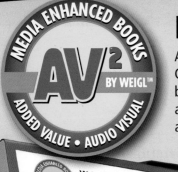

Log on to www.av2books.com

AV² by Weigl brings you media enhanced books that support active learning. Go to www.av2books.com, and enter the special code found on page 2 of this book. You will gain access to enriched and enhanced content that supplements and complements this book. Content includes video, audio, web links, quizzes, a slide show, and activities.

Audio
Listen to sections of the book read aloud.

Video
Watch informative video clips.

Embedded Weblinks
Gain additional information for research.

Try This!
Complete activities and hands-on experiments.

WHAT'S ONLINE?

Try This!	Embedded Weblinks	Video	EXTRA FEATURES
Test your knowledge of food chains.	Discover more carnivores.	Watch a video introduction to carnivores.	
Outline the features of an carnivore.	Learn more about one of the carnivores in this book.	Watch a video about a carnivore.	
Research a carnivore.	Find out more about carnivore conservation efforts.		
Compare carnivores that live in different areas.	Learn more about carnivores.		
Try an interactive activity.			

Audio
Listen to sections of the book read aloud.

Key Words
Study vocabulary, and complete a matching word activity.

Slide Show
View images and captions, and prepare a presentation

Quizzes
Test your knowledge.

AV² was built to bridge the gap between print and digital. We encourage you to tell us what you like and what you want to see in the future.

Sign up to be an AV² Ambassador at www.av2books.com/ambassador.

Due to the dynamic nature of the Internet, some of the URLs and activities provided as part of AV² by Weigl may have changed or ceased to exist. AV² by Weigl accepts no responsibility for any such changes. All media enhanced books are regularly monitored to update addresses and sites in a timely manner. Contact AV² by Weigl at 1-866-649-3445 or av2books@weigl.com with any questions, comments, or feedback.